Adventurize Your Summer!

Also by Chris Pannell

Drive
The Fragmentarium and Other Poems
Love, Despite the Ache
A Nervous City
Sorry I Spent Your Poem
Three Broadsheets of Poems
Under Old Stars

Adventurize Your Summer!

poems

Chris Pannell

Published by James Street North Books
an imprint of Wolsak and Wynn Publishers
280 James Street North
Hamilton, ON L8R2L3
www.wolsakandwynn.ca

Editor: Maureen Hynes | Copy editor: Ashley Hisson
Cover and interior design: Jennifer Rawlinson
Cover image: Photo by Janice Jackson, street artist unknown
Graffiti image: Diora Blesso/Vecteezy.com
Author photograph: Janice Jackson
Typeset in Adobe Caslon Pro
Printed by Coach House Printing Company, Toronto, Canada

10 9 8 7 6 5 4 3 2 1

The publisher gratefully acknowledges the support of the Ontario Arts Council, the Canada Council for the Arts and the Government of Canada.

Library and Archives Canada Cataloguing in Publication

Title: Adventurize your summer! : poems / Chris Pannell.
Names: Pannell, Chris, 1956- author.
Identifiers: Canadiana 20230184847 | ISBN 9781989496688 (softcover)
Classification: LCC PS8581.A64 A78 2023 | DDC C811/.54—dc23

I always love to begin a journey on Sundays, because I shall have the prayers of the church to preserve all that travel by land or by water.
    – Jonathan Swift, *Polite Conversation*, "Dialogue II"

Does the road wind up-hill all the way?
    Yes, to the very end.
Will the day's journey take the whole long day?
    From morn to night, my friend.
    – Christina Rosetti, "Up-Hill"

"Having adventures comes naturally to some people," said Anne serenely. "You just have a gift for them or you haven't."
    – L.M. Montgomery, *Anne of Avonlea*

Contents

Signs

I Am Graffiti

On boxcars and tankers
my colours jump as we pass the level crossing.
Clanging bells – it's been a long train.

So many city signs on poles (though confidentially
I find them rather conservative). That one points to the municipal dump.
That's my last mayor on the wall, says the recycling boss
as he takes out a fresh cigar.

The names of the old landmarks were changed
and those signs overpainted. The people
making new jobs for one another.

You might not know – but that building
used to be named for a former prime minister –
and here, around the back, is my private wall
a kind of notebook, full of complaints.

I'm losing track, afraid of the future.
We need someone who's in for the long haul, like this train.
Kids have been flinging stones into the bulrushes
but no one emerges. We could all use a guide.

The homeless push shopping carts up streets named Prosperity
or Lifestyle. If you trip over giant brass letters
set sideways in pavement, do not stop to read.

Let that phone in your hand go dark.
They can follow you when it's on. Take this.
It's a map. We used to call this stuff paper.
I'm here, deep in the folds.

I must make my mark, even though these
city corners have made me crazy. Get a pen
and a few spray cans of various colours. Some stencils,
some simple shapes. And we'll be off

to record the treason of our tongues, the tremor
of our talk.

The birds call

 and trill
screech, clatter
cluck across the universe of Trinity Church Road.
An occasional car
 Dopplers

 past –
the bird symphonics
 stop.
The bush rests. The tree fades.

They resume – call my heart out from its nest
between my lungs, under my ribs.

Come forward, bloody beating thing.
Tell us what you feel this Sunday
under heavy-to-rain clouds, where grey upon darker grey
bears down.

Blue jay catches my eye
as does the deep red cardinal –
the flitting flag of masculine fire.

The band resumes
curr-chunk, curr-chunk: pipple-mat
cargee, cargee, cargee, cargee.
Tweet (and again after some time waiting for it)
 tweet.

Are birds really our better selves,
with feathers? Our first solution for them
was the net, then the cage.
While others of the human kind – drugged or drunk
with the idea of flight –
launched themselves to know the air.
Exhausted, they fell.

Click. Cluck.
A chicken roams free of the barn. I lie on the ground.
Head cocked to one side, she leans over
silently mocks me.

Exit Through Ragged Falls

The warning sign about dangerous falls ahead
has been defaced.
Letters scraped free of their job
a canoeist's life
a signifier in the balance.

You can drift down slow
through this Algonquin afternoon,
the sun dappling golden leaves.
The water curves pastorally
into Ragged Falls.
You will be torn apart
one of nature's great moments:
death in a second of hang time
underwater, without air, words.

Signs have been hacked down all over.
The tallest trees produce the most shade,
the most oxygen for the largest number
but they were cut two hundred years ago
for Victoria's navy.

Explorers on their ships could smell the pines
as they approached North America.
It was an entirely different place.

The Captain's Voice

It's the beauty that thrills me with wonder,
The stillness that fills me with peace.
– Robert Service, "The Spell of the Yukon"

1.

From the port bow, the mountain is
a massive pair of dog paws at water's edge
ice white and grey with gravel.
Above, bared peaks sharpen the Alaskan air.

Meanwhile, the chatterbox of the intercom, the director of upsell
    repeats:
    We have tickets to wine tasting events!
    Don't miss tonight's musical stylings of Don Dinatello!
He doesn't report that too few pedicures and facials
have been sold on deck seven. He really wants to know
if the diamond shops in town got all your money today.

From steel speakers on the promenade deck, the captain's voice
volleys over the sleeping and the partying cruise patrons.
Marketing students in summer jobs learn the lingo.
    Nouns! Seize this chance to become a verb!
    Adventurize your summer!

2.

The story of the Klondike, like mountains and sky
is easy to grasp. It's a disappearance the locals are trying
to preserve. Greed, like dying for gold, has
bequeathed us a scenic railway.

Our enormous ship carefully drifts
into a dwindling supply of wilderness experiences.
We remain deaf to the silence, the lapping inlets
where otters and humpback whales know their way.

I am a page that would be free of this floating book –
one of many salmon that didn't make the spawning ground
and now lie dead, in the riverbed, or ashore, mauled by a bear
after the attempt.

Oh, the dull edge of having it all.
          (How excited I should be!)
See that *gravelanche*, scree down the mountainside?
By the milky green water of the bay,
silent, I will lie.

Father and son,

we face each other in the lounge of the long-term care home. No standoff. No gunslingers. His wheelchair against my cushioned armchair. I have brought his old corgi in hopes he might still be my father's beast, but Quincey points his cool wet nose away, toward the door. My father is a shocking portrait of my future. Having lived a non-smoking, moderate-alcohol, risk-free life longer than eighty years, he now embodies so many medical conditions he's encyclopedic: a teaching reference, a visual aid for med students, interns, oncologists. He says little and when he speaks he weaves between the stoic and emotional. He lists to one side, like a grounded ship – all his cargo slumping off decks into the bay. And yet there's as much fatherliness in him as ever. In silence and in words he pours his feelings everywhere. He inquires about my wife and my work. He seems tired of allocating and approving what his children are doing with his estate. What remains of his liveliness are his questions. When is your new book coming out? *I may not be around to see it.* What kind of bird is that, worrying at the window? *There's a lot I used to know.* Has Quincey been behaving himself? *I've come to realize there is nothing to be afraid of in dying.*

From Behind His Chair

In the days before television brought
its black-and-white soul home to us,
my father would read a book after dinner.
The book, as I stood behind his chair,
was made all the more interesting, because he never
let me finish a page. He would snap it shut
if I disturbed the dream of his imagination.
Don't read over my shoulder.

My soft breathing must have annoyed
away the imagery he had gathered –
and severed him from the writer's work –
to lay down through narrow conduits of understanding
what was already imagined, arranged and page-bound.

Trapped and airborne
at eighty-five percent of the speed of sound I am
sleepless overnight to Warsaw. The window:
portal to layers of darkness. Interior lights
illuminate my face.
I struggle
with the back of the seat before me,
its tiny internet of entertainments
bland movies, music and miniature dreams.
I fidget. Alone.

The plane's massive monotone has been engineered
to fragment thought, so each may compose their own torment.
And I'm deep in stroppiness without a father
to keep me calm. Only a destination, hours away
to crave.

At last returned to Earth, luggage in hand, how sweet
to stand and stretch and feel unbent from the seat

the confinement. Ready to be lit by the same sun rising
that set on our departure. Hundreds and hundreds released
from a strange word *cabin* – exhausted, on the tarmac of tomorrow.

Wary of Classical Music

The porcelain cameos of European composers
on the lid of our blue cookie tin
defined immortality when I was eight, though I was surely
too young to understand the notion of dying.

My father sat at the living room cabinet –
the turntable he'd wired into his radio
ready to accept the needle at the edge of the spinning vinyl.
His right hand rose above his head
to sustain a tremulous phrase in the strings
some slow passage of a Wagner prelude, some bright phrase in *Messiah*.
I was not to interrupt his thoughts, or clap
between symphonic movements or after the soprano's aria.
Like an orchestra, I was obedient
to the way a conductor's fingers can close off a note.

We attended few concerts.
More often, in the living room, in comfy chairs
we attended the melodies and harmony –
but lately, not wanting to think of him more often than I must
I don't listen to classical music much anymore.

It's too late of course to become indifferent
to the sonata, a concerto or even a bagatelle.
Having once been commanded by Herbert von Karajan,
by ballets and opera
I cannot turn back.

My father had been a dedicated singer in the company choir.
I incline my head to the stereo system and turntable he later bought.
I cannot forget him for a moment through
all fifty-six minutes of *Eroica* – like a premonition
carries me through the themes and their many variations –
as Beethoven became aware of his approaching deafness.

Young pianists and violinists can still seduce
with their costumes, their languid fingering and
stabbing strokes with the bow.
We used to turn to each other, from time to time
and smile at the same astonishing passage, the acoustics of a church,
the genius of a sound engineer.

He taught me to have opinions
and later, when I found myself working in the massive
main store of Sam the Record Man, I knew
how to advise the customer which was the best of fifty
different versions of Vivaldi's *Four Seasons* in the Schwann catalogue.

My father died without a Requiem, or the pathos
of *Amadeus*. His finale was austere, to lie between
beige and green walls, flat on his back
on a mechanical bed. When he told me
he was not afraid of dying
did I nod?

His eyes closed, but he spoke,
thanked me for visiting him.
I waited until Strauss's "Blue Danube" had ended,
then took the disc from the player
and put it ever so carefully away.

Temporal Loss

On a velvet table
slow billiard balls – click.
Clues pile up about a man we know
who is losing himself – entropy all round.
Downstream, in rubber boots, we follow
these creeks, take paths that used to clearly cross
the certainties we hold.

We've heard his unshaven ideas, seen his stained shirts
mad scribbles, the clusters of fallen hair. He evades
us like a gusty wind sweeping leaves from the steps
of his home. The wet newspapers, house foundations
crooked. His kitchen counter
covered with old meals: dishes stinking, cutlery
disposable plastic.

No turning away.
Sometimes we feel
his ghost in tight orbit around our fears.
With chins upturned, we watch Banquo above the banquet.
He challenges us, his sisters and
hopeless brothers, blames us for his death –
while he lives.

The present, an unfunny joke –
while the past he knows is a rich tapestry of pleasure,
like a mouthful of fruitcake. Erect within himself
his wisdom hidden, his sins locked up
where they can do no harm.

We search the larger and longer spaces, our hands comb the air,
then fall to our own responsibilities.

He is the silver bauble we let slip
from the broken necklace of our family.
Only at night do we hear his dreamlike rage –
the hollering of a lost hunter,
echoes of his former life.

I Read All Twelve Signs

My new temp job at the university
is to exercise in public
with a mail cart, to roll down corridors
Excuse me! through crowds, throngs, gaggles
though I fear being seen
below my station
vain of my education
like a disgraced stockbroker
working off his sentence in community service
I fear a chance encounter with Profs Perkin or Jones.

Economics is cyclical
and the newspaper suggests better jobs are ahead
but only out of town
waiting is the hardest part, unless it's searching
unless it's rejection, unless it's the horoscope
speaking to those who require straws to clutch –
I read all twelve signs.

Partners are faithful though you are filled with doubt.
Today Aries and Capricorn are to receive raises
Aquarius, Taurus and Scorpio will be shortchanged
Gemini, Libra and Pisces will form
a romantic attachment
with wealth. The horoscope author

has an interest in interest
that carries over to the Report on Business
which prints all the rates for every currency creature
nesting in pockets and vaults.

The horoscope: a fantasy of journalism.
The long poem: a form of university life
losing energy in the later pages
particle physics describes how
speed and collision lead to fission
like hundreds of undergrads let out to flirt in the
spring sunshine.
Cutbacks have slowed the tandem accelerator
so now it merely speeds and radiates
smash atom, smash on.

The lawns and gardens are wet with melt,
earth holds water like a sponge of grass.
Keys from maples and crabapple trees
brown febrile letters
a whole word here and there
a van drives by and
      1-800-LAWN – We'll make you green
such bliss
                  fuzzy headed and the glass tipped over
              I am escaped into my own dream
that friends and lovers know I'm suffering
and are looking to bring me back
from the life of a servant to academe.

Here I hide
in a storeroom with high windows
scribbling, shirking the delivery
of books and journals, the papers and Post-it Notes of genius.

Let's digress to Wordsworth's mad notion in *Lyrical Ballads*
that Nature is the God of Man
that crackling English-centricity can seem
quite a shock if you bring it forward too quickly
from those old school days
when chums were thrashed by perverted headmasters.
Oh, we don't do that anymore
say the professors of progress
and me hiding in this lying-under-a-tree pose
and it is spring, a not-so-terrible April with buds on trees
and after months of worry
and a cheque forthcoming.

Not such a cruel month after all
though we'll get to Good Friday soon enough
and also Easter's redemption.

A Statue Speaks in Lisbon

Please –
your coins for my hat of dreams.

Oh you, the people!
      You do not see me apply the paint to my face, create the tarnish
      for the hat on my head, and my jacket. Such an illusion –
You are not privy to my chemistry or my dressing room.
My copper complexion shimmers green, down over the fabric
of my trousers and even my shoes.

Look to my second hat, below my plinth.
Its silk liner hides the few euros I could have spent on breakfast.
You flocked to Florence to see Michelangelo's *David* do nothing.
You have paid and paid to see
that piece of marble
imitate the ideal man.

But at eighty-eight kilos
my hunger weighs more, though marble, long ago
mastered the stillness. My mother says
You have raised the doing of nothing to a high art.

On columns, you raised sculptures
      of generals, prime ministers and queens.
In gratitude you placed their faces on stamps
        on paper money.

What might make you make a statue of me
for pretending for years
to be a stone in your public square?
When will you install my face on the facades
of a building where you shelter or work?
Do not whine, my mother said.
Suffering is part of the human condition.

And that's my pain, to move and be thought
a poor performer, a silent song, a sonnet without sentiment.
Try to be still – you just try – while from this harbour
explorers left, some never to return.
            Here I want to thump my chest, for effect –
while every man who pretends to be a statue
eventually quits the job because he aches to move.

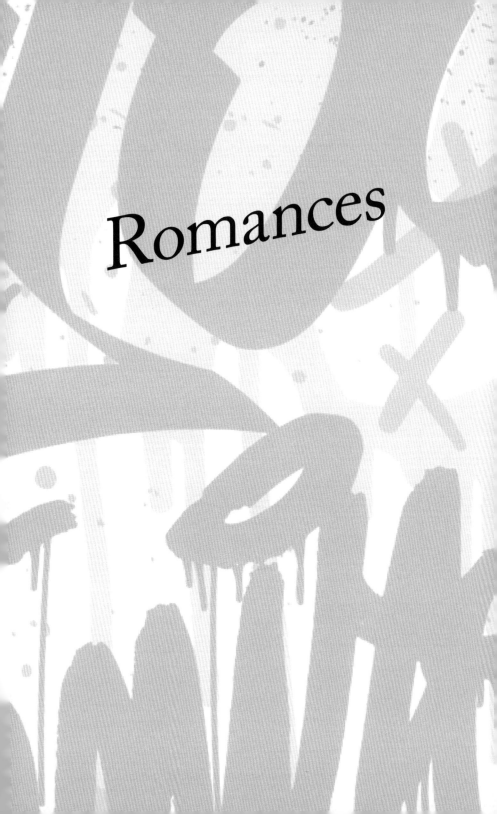

Romances

Le Lit (The Bed)

after a painting by Henri de Toulouse-Lautrec

Half-concealed –
two figures gaze at each other
eyes narrowing on sleep
their hair like tangled thoughts.

Soft pillow points arch out
against the bridge carved in the headboard
and join them in bliss.

Read the red duvet, the vertical grains in the wood.
Like waves, their sheets suggest the horizon
while blue and yellow brushstrokes
whisper
      lie down.

The peace and pleasure of a bed
appeals to the footsore traveller in Paris.

Under cover, a hand reaches
      from left to right
a gesture of *need* and *gift*
      and when the right returns her affection
their smiles will mirror
the warmth between them.

We have barely –

        oh –

      touches of pink and red betray
what the duvet doesn't hide.

      We mean you no harm,
lovers.

Water Lilies

for Janice Jackson

The tour group scatters across
my view of the pond like raucous brown
and blue leaves. One incessant giggler
cannot be still. Two of her teenage friends
stand shoulder to shoulder, try to hide her.
The rest slow and gather, chatter
and carelessly attend the echo of their guide
who speaks
in sharp tones.

They are here to check
this attraction off their list.
The climate control at l'Orangerie
is far too subtle to affect
these twelve around our seat.

Begone! I want to roar.
That I might sit selfishly with Monet's
curves! The walls, the work –
that I might fall into his mind with my astonishment.

My teeth clench, then your warm fingers
and the invisible sun
touch my aching back, and reassure me
of the clouds.

I remember Ophelia –
how John Everett Millais kept her alive
      afloat in a bower of green, brightly erotic.

Today, Monet's pond and sky are blessing blue
and absent the girl, he brings to mind the living
lilies and bamboo
of Giverny
yesterday.

Painted fronds move or am I moved
to see reflections of them in those clouds?
I float on the surface of all things
under shadow of willow
on wounds received
by rushing through
      what we came for
        and might love
          if only we would consider.

The tour group begins to leave
their guide is speaking English: *Keep up, keep up!*

Time and my eyes widen on the foliage,
fronds. Weeds and puckers of pink,
deep greens underwater, under skin
seem to snare and submerge us
(Ophelia, again). Blooms pop white –
rush in from riverbank, from the sky
to save us. So many places to rest
dans le jardin d'eau.

By the Portrait of
a Polish Nobleman

On the squeaking heels of new shoes
a visitor to Washington
comes and goes, to see and know.
His blue windbreaker billows
as he moves. His back
blocks my view of Rembrandt's portrait –
he leans

way too close
to the authority and sadness of this Polish man.
The viewer's pointed nose and grey hair say
he's mature. He wears expensive name brands.
He has put in over forty years at the same company in San Jose
or Boston, at over a hundred thousand
per year – and there'll be no getting rid of him.
Yet he's frustrated
by this canvas, by the look of the Polish nobleman and
he's thinking of asking Larry about it
Larry who knows art so well
Where is he?

He swivels, scans the room, *Hey, Larry!*
What do you make of this Polish thing?
Hunger, for more than
the sitter or Rembrandt
will say in paint, more than he grasps.
The more I look the less sense this makes.
Then, still blocking my view
he gestures to the women across the room –
perhaps his wife is chatting
with Larry's wife. She does not come.
Or hear. One must not shout
in the National Gallery of Art.

The bearskin with the golden chain,
the glistening earring, the fur,
the sitter's soft secure grip on his staff
show how warm light centres
Rembrandt's frame.
The bright and dark, a division
of his face into good
and almost evil, or perhaps
his vulnerability. What he would say in Polish
through his ruddy cheeks, slightly open lips
about the difficulty of sitting
for Rembrandt those long hours?

The viewer blurts
It seems so damn progressive!
then covers his mouth, he sags
sees his glasses have been smudged all day, he straightens
like the Boy Scout he was forty years ago,
harrumphs his final confidence.

Rembrandt's light entraps us
brown and grey, swaths of white and cream
seem to swirl and then
even the wall behind the Polish nobleman
glows, as if there had been electricity
four hundred years ago, in that studio.

Air swells to a gust
then stops. The security guard – white shirt with crests
and two-way radio – on tired feet and knees
moves to his seat in the next room.
He doesn't hear
the visitor to the National Gallery of Art
fall to the floor.

Red Hill Sumacs

Far into the valley
rain hits the sumacs along the Red Hill Creek
settles to earth, into the slow stream.
There's no galvanized culvert yet
but the road will be built
so the friends of city hall may have
their expressway, jobs and money.

In the sunny afternoon, mud smears
make clear the path
construction trailers will follow
not far from the hikers' path.
The raccoon sleeps away the day in a tree
the eagle circles high
looks for mice, random life.

Soon we will have standards:
lanes, rules of road, noise and light
at night, everything done for the purpose
of getting somewhere else, of being gone from here.

The creatures are here. They have no desire to leave
while the sumacs bleed in the autumn sun
and asphalt is an abstraction
still to come.

At the top of the food chain stands
a high school student who works Sundays at the burger bar,
a destination so transitory it might as well be a dream.

But if she should ever pause in her order-taking
let it be because the pheasant and the wolf
have wandered in and are about to escape
between the buildings on either side
with whatever part of the human place setting
strikes their fancy, and can be shared
with their young.

The Staircase and the Young

They tear by me
as if they can climb to the stars
laugh at the view of the town below
when they get there.

Short of breath, shaky legs.
I climb these stairs
to prove I still can,
to keep my distance from burial grounds.

Dusk at the top of the escarpment
restores me from my fear
of half-shadows
from the way my writing hand with pen
has turned grey, a shade toward
the off-white of dying senses
the slow consumption of the fire
that burns in every evening star.

The Rain, Her Crutches and Fireworks on Victoria Day

On the boulevard
       a boy carries his girl high on his back.
Her breasts
against the back of his neck
she is all arms and clammy clutch –
with every step her fresh white cast bobs
hangs to one side and
tucked between them, her crutches
make a crossbeam.

A Roman candle flares behind a neighbour's hedge
                 then a rocket
screams   up   up

over the maples, thick cedars barricade a deep yard
               a green   ka-pock
overhead
               a shower of
embers fade to white and out of sight
like the Queen, this night, abstract.

Bearded clouds have held back
for hours, now let down the drizzle.

FLASH of lightning
(pause)
hard Crash roars through the sky
                         then
              all is calm   all is night
lush backyards and parks echo
what the thunder said
         a smaller crash

The boy pauses, to catch breath –
she squeezes him, her soldier –
He imagines a sergeant's voice, an urging to
Maintain stance!
                  He squats, adjusts
his grip under her thighs, hoists her higher
his arms behind
Resume March!

                  He's both steed and knight
that strains to match the might
of St. Christopher.

Rain streams across their faces
drums on the hoods of cars
thrashes the surfaces of puddles –

then slowly
        the storm begins to slacken.
Our drenched pair
shuffles through the urban green
and dark, approaches the headlights
that catch her pine crutches
her bobbing cast like a beacon
and her draping hair hangs wet
over his shoulder,
giggle and breath on his neck.

One last CRACK, another Rrrrummmble
and the towering clouds
seem to part, the rain lessens. Soon –
only drops in the night
from trees and troughs.

They are almost home.

A poem takes the shape

of the paper
a roll of adding machine tape, a paper bag
       torn open.
When our breath condenses
we write with fingers on the car's windshield
love notes to be lost when we drive off –
our names air-conditioned away.

The machinery directs so much
and we
the rude mechanicals, let it go on effacing us –
the poet knows he is nothing
but memory and flesh –
a few disappointments about to enter unconsciousness
where past generations have flown, aglow.

The happy couple's prenuptial party in June
was blessed by pouring rain and hundreds of hungry souls.
The tractor was driven
by her younger brother. Her grinning uncle
watched the towing chain draw tight –
they pulled cars from the muddy field all night.
Wet and spinning tires, a struggle
but the timing perfect – like the inside of this bag, at hand
for thinking about the future, while the couple commits
to their future
on a hilltop, in a leaking tent.

We shrink under the threats of weather
and think of what we need to build
or fix in our shelter. Some things cannot wait
for better days. Brown paper, wrinkled, water-spotted
flat upon my knee – my windshield fogged and clouded
seems fortunate. A Caribbean honeymoon forthcoming.
Bare feet warm
and tingling on the sand.

Field Guide to the Kootenay Mountain Tourist

The Eastern Migrating Tourist is a plentiful creature that travels rapidly in small herds through Western North America from May to September. It has no natural enemies except others of its own kind. Typically, the male drives, the female plans and instructs. A video camera replaces the television remote control commonly used for conflict escalation and resolution in their natural habitat.

In herds, tourists frolic in the results of the planet's volcanic and core upheavals, collect pebbles and are greatly amused by magnifying their vision with glass and capturing imagery. Plants and animal species endure displacement and declining numbers. For mammals, there is a deadly risk of socialization from repeated contact. Additionally, animal habitats can accumulate dangerous quantities of tourist effluent and foodstuffs dispelled from high-speed or stationary travel devices.

Rain or fire are the only forces that can reliably dispel this species. Even bad weather, however, has no effect if they migrate in packs or use large flying machines. In flight they seem almost benign, as distant as the clouds; as difficult to encounter as a snowy mountain peak. Migration in these modes is preferred as it is least obtrusive, and has caused year-round residents of the Kootenay to sometimes think of the tourists as a wisp of distant, concealed life.

An Alaskan Refugee

The metal detector and the cruise ship security guards
did not see him leave. Silent footfalls,
midnight moon, steel gangway.

In the morning, a stream of clothes through the passageways –
an open suitcase by the elevators. His last purchases
(according to finance) were unpaid: a glass of beer, a blue baseball cap
bearing the stars of Alaska's flag.

Perhaps the admonitions of perky stewards and waiters
to have fun did not convince. They were always working.
He went to bed early, not ready for the adventure of his life

and the hazards of the world's largest temperate rainforest –
the wisdom of rocks, the speed of glaciers, fresh snow.

The cruise director was taken to the mainland for questioning.
We all have experienced a change of plans.
Ship: stationary.
Harbour water: brackish green.
Passengers should be accounted for
not lost along the way.

The dining room menus shrank, supplies ran out
including fuel for the engines. Eventually thousands were released
ashore to survey end-of-season souvenirs and mediated frontiers.

Perhaps he packed himself, shipped himself home
where he could be alone with squirrels and cats.
Or perhaps that's him – carving his likeness
into one of the deep limestone valleys
around Glacier Bay. Perhaps
he was never here at all.

A Dog's Poem

I am a creature of the earth.
What matters is the smell of the world
that aroma from which we came, that smell
I lead you to.

My master has a very short nose that seems
not to work. He's ignorant of so many
things around him. I try to point out the pee
and shit and flowers and the dead mouse over there
and all the rest. Sticks and branches. From time to time
I like to chew. I learn by tasting the plants –
garbage is life.

He's very impatient, though he has time to take
me out four times a day. Sometimes he puts a leash on me
sometimes not. I don't care. Leashes get in the way.
He walks the leash; I carry the other end of it.
Wear it yourself, if you like it so much. Ask any dog.

Don't care much for talk. A game I don't play –
Growl, woof, yelp and moan, that's about it.
He waves his hands.
He talks to me a lot. Unless he's angry or sad or lost or lonely
then he goes quiet. I get bored when he talks to other people.
But I'd rather him than anyone else.

I feel peculiar when his voice rolls out slowly
and he gently touches me, rubs me. I need him,
but I don't belong to him.
He feeds me and so do others we live with. His wife,
for example.

They all ignore the earth – ask any dog
they have no idea what they are walking on. How much
they can learn from it, what is dangerous, what is safe.
I know.
He should dawdle.
Get down on all fours, chew the grass where it's long.
Roll on his back from time to time
rub his face on the ground.
He'd pick up the sweetest smells and carry them
on his pants, all through the day.
In winter, I have to wait a long time while he dresses
at the front door, before we go out.
His scarf is not a toy for tugging.
His gloves are not for chewing.
His sweater, his coat, his hat, his wallet, his keys, those bags
he uses to pick up poop. I mean why?
It's crazy to be picking up poop all the time.
Ask any dog.

It would be easier if he had fur
to carry all the smells from the ground.
Oh well.
I am a creature of the earth. The birds are creatures of the air.
My master cannot fly, he cannot smell, he has slow reactions, sometimes
I have to bark at him. It's hard to figure what he's good at
he's too slow to chase a squirrel –
but somehow he's very good at finding food.

Give credit where it's due.
I feel his love when he puts food in my bowl
on the floor, when he washes my dishes and refills the water.
Faithfully.

Good master, good boy.

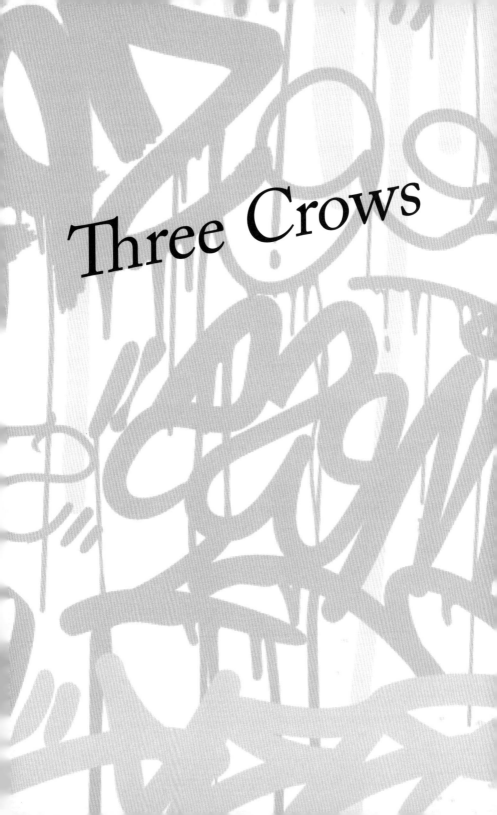

Three Crows

One Frozen Foot

he limps along King Street

one winter, he took no medication
stayed out five nights in a row
his right foot now bare plastic
toes chipped and broken
left running shoe worn down

his constant cigarette leads the way
purple sweater rides up
scratches his distended belly
> *let them stare –*
> *this torn overcoat and cane*
> *disguise me from those Nazis*

soon it will be dusk and laundry night at the home
> *I can't stay where the walls talk*
> *the army corps of engineers are coming*
> *dynamite through the house*
> *they're coming tonight*
> *gonna detonate my room like they did before*
> *and the house before the house before*

High Command so cunning
to blow up the home of their own agent
there will be a dossier drop and some gold
at one bus stop or the other

last year a driver threw him off the bus between
Sanford and Wentworth

> *that double agent bears watching*
> *British intelligence expects*
> *every spy will do his duty*

someone's coming in the dark with a flashlight
a familiar face

> *shall I elude him*
> *or just play dumb?*

For the Trainee Bus Driver

Let's begin with the Song of the Fire Extinguisher
     Please release me, let me go
     I'm so cold in this red can
     so compressed while the world burns for me
     I could be much more
          than foam.

And here come the safety triangles
escapees from the orchestra's pay-attention section
     a ding, ding   *ding-a-ling*
larger than you'd expect, when they are strung out
     along Highway Eight, diverting traffic.
Merge left, you fools.

And consider the whole DARTS bus now:
a giant doodad of belts and wheels
fluids, pistons, fenders and heat.
Toss those people and things in the back
and let's get going, on schedule –
     a one-two-three, one-two-three
except when you break down,
your schedule blown,
for example, by a tire.

The working day will be a waltz
or a footrace or a walk in the park.
You'll learn to follow your nose
to sniff the map, heed Dispatch, to swear
and find passengers by street name and landmark –
a string of stops across the city.
Sometimes (but rarely)
over the roar of the engine
you'll hear them speak to you.

Though you've just begun,
they've been trying to get your attention for years.

How We Fear Each Other

Tonight, Franceska is well-dressed
her hair coiffed, the ideal mature woman
in a wheelchair, who hates her wheelchair –
and told me so last week. Tonight, she'll cry
all the way from family dinner at her son's house
back to Idlewyld Manor.

Along the way, we stop at a nondescript group home
with no romantic name
to pick up a handsome young man who might
have been an athlete in another life
who staggers slowly up the steel ramp of the DARTS bus.
He grunts and yelps, his heavy boots clank the pauses
in his progress.

At last, soaked from the rain, he enters into the light –
no sloppy charisma, no charming grin to ease his way.
I try to guide him to a place behind her.
For ten seconds, his feet won't move –
then he can't bend at the waist. Face furious and rigid
his head and hands flail and I'm weighed down
with his overnight bag. I duck one of his elbows
and in the end, he falls into
the seat I wanted him to fall into
loudly hollers his pleasure at not having hit his head
on a handrail or the floor.
A wordless boy who tries to converse.

Franceska stops sobbing.
Do you have to take him?
I buckle his seat belt. Victor grins, stares away
then watches me return to the driver's seat.

Easter Sunday: full moon, obscured by clouds.
For a moment, I forget where we're going
until I see the company's schedule
with the addresses.

Franceska bows her head, dabs her eyes with
a handkerchief, perfumed with strawberry –
            her new life shames her.
Victor so unlike her moneyed sons and daughters
and polite society
he might as well be on the moon.

The bus rolls on, Victor howls, almost in rhythm with our wheels
toward our next stop: his mother's house where she admits
him one night of every weekend.
When his mother dies, then what?
What can we do for boys who speak like Victor?
Who feel the world as we cannot?

Franceska is crying again –
for the taste of veal, dolmades and wine.
I slow to hear quiet laments
that wash down her pain in the dark.

I accelerate to hear Victor,
his urgent grunts, his warning to not
be afraid, lest
we all find ourselves under water.

First Bus Out on a Sunday Morning

Three crows in a tall spruce –
the waning crescent moon hangs low at dawn –
a bauble, symbolic of all disappointments
like getting up early for work.

Empty city streets will soon act out
their little dramas. Night stars recede
into sirens on Upper James.

Streetlights wink off, the two-way radio
is silent.

The crows have begun to bicker
to jostle, replace one another in
the cone-laden highest branches.
There is enough room
for three but no crow shares top spot.
Suddenly
something in their global view of things –
all three
languidly
swoop down on a mouse
foolish enough to explore
the edge of grass and parking lot.

Behind the mass of thrashing feathers and mouse
an arrow on a concrete wall
directs the absent traffic about to park
one way, the right way home for cars laden
with treasure hunted from stores.

The birds have separated in all directions, none with the prey
who must have escaped under a shrub. Two crows alight
on the concrete wall. They prance and caw at the third
who stabs and waddles in the ruffled grass.
City winds are amplified, heavy branches sway
a car throbs past and building glass clatters –
exhales the smudge of a black, overdriven
bass guitar.

On Concession Eight West at Dusk

The clouds over fields make fans
and a vortex. A purple sky turns slow black.

We are ninety-eight percent water
moving at sixty kilometres per hour in a bus
susceptible to the heavier winds and potholes.

One day, we'll rejoin the water cycle as if
we were only ever participants in a storm –
after a life of holding up, in this other form.

James is weak, with a headache, unable
to muster the volume of voice to be irritable.

His wheelchair gleams blue and chrome
like a naval officer's jacket, but he's haggard.

A former trucker, he talks less on the way home
from dialysis than he ever has before –
too weak even for back-seat driving.

Goddess, when you take to the sky tonight
take what remains of James in your arms.

Passenger Paul, Three Trips on DARTS

1.

The first night I was assigned to be a meds driver
Paul was on board,
he saved my shift and my nascent career as a bus driver –
instructed me how to get him
and those four other cranky passengers
home in the right sequence, as quickly as possible, through
rush hour, gridlock, where nothing moves and it always takes
longer than an hour.
An ex-cabbie, an ex-dispatcher,
he knows Hamilton
every street, every corner, every dumb idea.

2.

Next, I met him on Christmas Eve –
he was practically falling to the floor from low blood sugar,
his wife trying to strap him up
with a belt around his sunken chest,
but the back of his wheelchair was too short.
And everyone on the bus wondered
if he would make the forty-minute trip
– to St. Joe's, for dialysis.
I suggested an ambulance. She said
it would take too long, to unload him,
to make the call, to wait for them to come and then

the trip. She shoved a little chocolate between his lips,
he stirred.

3.
Two days into January, he's binding his stump as if this is hockey
and a skate lace has broken. A clean tensor bandage.
Shaved for the new year, for this sunny, bitter cold morning.
His voice fills the bus,
as happy as a curmudgeon can be,
discussing the city, the idiots on council,
the new year, the future of downtown – like he believes in the future.
He straightens up on his scooter – something interests him
in the conversion of one-way streets
back to two directions.

Let's roll, Paul – find us a map and a ramp
up the steps of city hall –
we'll circle the evergreens with lights
and say we'll never leave.

One Morning, One Afternoon

This morning, in the bookstore of the Library of Congress
I browse an anthology of forty-three poet laureates
of the United States of America. Foreword by Billy Collins.

This afternoon at the National Gallery
I spy someone rowing a boat through
the lower right corner of Rembrandt's *The Mill*.

My wife admires the windmill catching
late afternoon sun on three of its four blades.
There are clouds, but no wind.

She says the paint has likely faded since Rembrandt's day.
The background tends to brown, the sky to white.
Two men wait close to the shoreline to tie up the boat

its mast down and sails stowed.
A figure with a child waits further up the embankment.
Is that Billy Collins? I ask.

I hope his boat is slowing – the flag droops
and the mast looks
like it might collide with the foundation of the mill

or impale one of the swains on shore
trying to help. I should relax. Once upon a time this landscape
sang in shades of yellow, green and red – as various

as the anthology of laureates and Mr. Collins
and the brushes of Rembrandt van Rijn.
Doomed to fade while outlining what was.

Enriching this day. Pastoral Holland.
Energetic Billy at the oars.

The House Across the Street

is on drugs

at night it cries out
a voice like a thunderclap

then all is quiet
a few syringes fall
lightly on the neighbours' lawns
like rain

we are roused from sleep by a curse
and a threat drifts past our open window
a strange feeling of
stars under my eyelids
bright and sharp
illuminating
pain

A Month of Sundays

When the monster truck comes up the street
I know it's garbage day.
Otherwise, like Sundays, all days are the same.

I want a refund on my eventless calendar
stifled by a pandemic, by our rules of what not
to do, to keep me alive and all of you reading this.
(It must have worked, but for a few million here and there.)

Every sunrise the same, every gathering dusk.
        (What does it gather?)
Can I make of tomorrow as much (and little) as yesterday?
Trapped in false conflict: a meeting-less life, no opposition
to my thoughts, nowhere to go, as if we were sadder babes
to be delivered to bed, all day.

Winds rise and clear the skies, make a beauteous
sign of the cost of busyness, of industry.

Though now we crawl, be not a fatalist.
Reach for love. Think of pursuing what you do not know.
(Ah, you may not pursue it.) Evade what's viral, evade
the day to die, sooner than later.

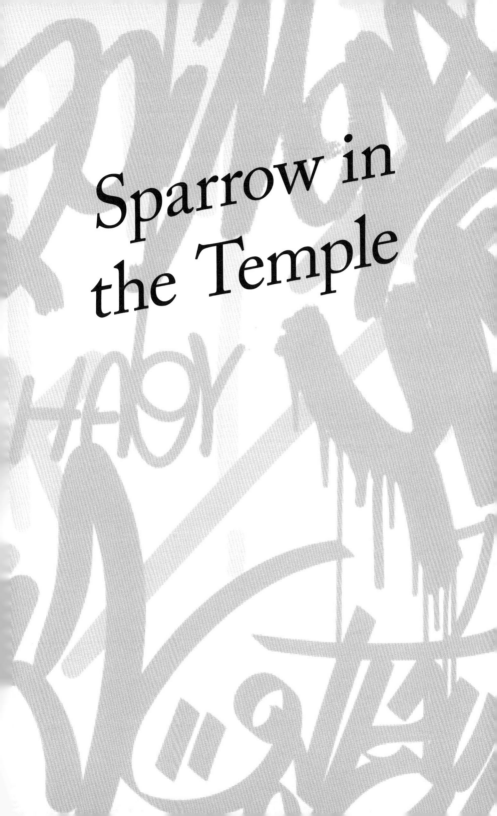

Sparrow in the Temple

A dream of being lost in Rome

the inks on my map blotched and ran
the motorways rose and fell like roller coasters
singing choruses from *Pagliacci*,
German and English signs
had been broken and tossed aside,
gargoyles on buildings dressed in suits
leapt down to the roads
and began to commandeer
red double-decker buses from
their streetcar tracks.

I was driving a taxi full of hit men
who were expecting me to get them quickly to
their destination
and to outwit the carabinieri.

In a Portuguese Botanical Garden

I try to rest but the barbed grass
tears at my skin – naked I lie
on its parched effort to survive.

I am tired of my pursuit, of incessant grieving
without relief of my love for you.

Mother, last night
I floated above your estates in disarray:
crumbling walls, sinkholes, emptiness.

In the heat of afternoon sun
I have watched cold ocean waves crash ashore.
The ship you sailed is gone forever,
its tattered masts, handsome sailors,
brothers of yours.

Tonight, my tears scatter fresh seeds
into the wet earth. In bright moonlight

I have grown beyond these garden fences.
I will be an oasis, spread across
the dry plain of your absence
softening, clarifying –

to exhale and sleep.

Cathedrals

There was only one story to tell.
They told it over and over, assuming it was right –
Solemn, frightening
assisted by illustrations in stained glass.

For the people were illiterate
and most days were sunny
and this was a complicated, unreal kind of story –
trying to understand the plan, which involved
seeing a world of suffering as God saw it –
and not with the happy grounding of a dog.

Many wandered away.
It was time to harvest, it was time to plant.
A cow had become ill and the oracle
had to be consulted. Father needed
a new tunic and shoes before winter.

They wrote in learned ways about gradations of beauty
and the levels of hell.
Privileged young men vied
to be the priest or an abbot.
No warning seemed to work
except putting someone
to death as an example.

The Nile

Egypt is the gift of the Nile.
– Herodotus

At forty thousand feet the plane is crunched
in thrusts of air, tossed like prey in the mouth
of a cat, until we are released onto the runway,
as from God's angry hand. We bounce, roll,
feel the concrete seams and wonder if these are
merely His Claws. *Thanks for sparing our lives.*

Modern airports, hypostyle temples –
everything will be shaken, struck.
Only the Nile never cracked. Even after Aswan,
an engineer's dream of controlling her indifference
to famine – she continued, made Lake Nasser,
a monument to herself. She has carried the living
on her skirt so long – among the floating bottles and bales
the dead cow floating off the bow of our cruise ship.

Ra warms, then burns and finally hobbles with a cane
at dusk. Everything else – that tree, that crocodile
the donkey before the cart – comes with a smallish soul.
At night we shed the clothes of infidels
become naked images afoot in the sand
watch Ra fall beneath the flat western edge of the world.
He will be reborn as a tiny scarab in the morning.

There are flies and whip marks on the horses' hindquarters.
The Nile has heard our pity. She invites the desert wind,
like Mark Antony, to build a new
empire on the eastern shore.

We are told how the second Rameses died, his greatness
a story for guides to recount, a matter of national pride.

How Alexander of Macedon, Greek king and brilliant soldier,
was killed by a germ in Iraq. *He was an arrow shot toward death.*
A moment of pain, whispers the Nile.

What remains are monuments and anecdotes of immortality
like rain gathered from southern sources.
Nothing we can carry
or cherish once we are home.

Sparrow in the Temple

From a seam in a sandstone wall
he shouts and cajoles
like the street vendors along the way.

His fellows and females, loyal lovers
gather in late afternoon at their nests –
tiny tunnels between the stones, where their chicks hatch
twice a year within Luxor and Karnak.

In the pause between every screech and tweet
the sparrow turns his head
seeking the gift she is. Cut into stone
at his left – Horus, the falcon god.
To his right, seven servants with a coffin
above; egrets, chariots, bountiful harvests
below, a princess with the head of a cat.

Where is she?

What Egypt built Alexander conquered
(the sparrows saw this too)
and after the Greeks came the Romans and among them
a Christian flood of unbelievers who scratched and chipped away
at the evil hieroglyphs.

His flashing eye is soft and tough. His flock
a thrashing flourish, their wings fluttering grey.
Bursting browns, flecked with granite black
release feathered fury over the sculpted heads of pharaohs
former commanders of these chambers.

Once upon a magic time
the sparrow would have told us to endure
to look with purpose on everything
before the sand wraps tourists and vendors of knickknacks
to sleep with the dead.

He pops back
into the dark between the stones.
She lands where he stood, follows, head first.
Her tail opens like a fan, as she disappears
into the small of the night.

Brief Egyptian Rain

1.

Hot   inert
      that city in the desert
pauses
         for
the drop in air pressure

    (then)

a three-minute torrent of flooding
makes pandemonium among the people.

Winds of power
a whip to the back. And again.
     The Goddess is here
         and gone.

On our skin, the welcome peace
of humidity
a breeze through our robes.
She pursues someone else after the rain.

2.

On a Nile cruise, time has nothing to say
about how it is used. All is drift, this aged
ship on which we've lived for days.

As if by magic, my wife becomes a pharaoh's queen
and I, a trader of corporations, owner of gold mines
a potentate of railcars full of oil.

Because I am white and I can speak complex sentences
in English, all this – though I do not mention
at home I am a school bus driver.

The Land of Many Gods

There is a god or spirit in every living thing
even the hippopotamus. Have mercy on me, Set!
Ferocious creature of the Nile, but you are also
our female goddess and protector of pregnant mothers.

Anubis, jackal-headed
guardian of graves and cemeteries
god of embalming, keeper of the scales
to weigh the heart of the dead and guide
of those whose souls are light enough to enter
the afterlife.

Geb, you laugh and the earth quakes
and our crops grow.
Primeval divine king, who gave us Osiris, your son,
and Horus, your grandson, who inherited the land.
Geb, you were married to Nut, the sky
but separated by Shu, the air.
Geb, a man reclining, with his penis
still pointing to heaven.

Ra dies every night. An afternoon of aging
he goes down in orange aura and dwells twelve hours
with Osiris, in the underworld. Ra travels in his boat –
to protect his fires from the primordial waters. For all our sakes.
In the morning he comes as a scarab, emerging
through Nut. He calls every creature into being
by speaking its name.
So the day begins.

A Cruise Ship in the Locks Between Luxor and Edfu

Water roars through huge concrete sluices back to the Nile.
In the desert, nothing is more precious.
Trapped between wet walls
our ship descends deeper and deeper –
there is no bottom, the day quickly
disappears, as if we are being swallowed by a huge serpent.

We lie on cabin beds
wrists crossed on our chests.
We have fallen from the surface of the world –
will miss Amun-Ra dying at dusk
when his solar boat passes west, above us.
Wrapped in layers of linen
our blood will drain, our bodies
will be preserved for us for the afterlife.

Kept alive only by the clever words of the captain –

> Remember the world, from which you came
> this ship, an enormous engine
> hinge and gear, propellers and fuel. Once you walked
> on polished wooden decks.

Do not fear the night
The sun will be reborn, as surely
as the Nile floods and narrows and floods again
in her fertility.

As priests inspired the people over thousands of years
to serve Misr and her kings, to build monuments
and temples. Stones were carved with iron tools
until, time's agents, the wind and sand
covered it all.

In the beginning,

Osiris the king loved Isis, but his brother Set became jealous and he crafted a jewelled coffin, made exactly to the king's dimensions. He offered it to all the nobles, none of whom it fit, until at last Osiris was seduced to lie in the coffin, which was slammed shut and nailed and sealed with lead. Set's accomplices threw it into the Nile.

Isis searched all of Egypt, and after many days, found the dead Osiris and buried him. Then Set, first god of the underworld, dug up the coffin and cut Osiris's body into thirteen pieces and scattered the pieces along the banks of the Nile. Witnesses told Isis of this and again she frantically searched the length of Egypt – the entire river. At last she found twelve parts of his body, which she wrapped in linen and made of him Egypt's first mummy.

Isis begged Anubis, the jackal-headed god, to bring Osiris back to life but Osiris could never be human again, for his penis had been eaten by a fish that resembled Set, so Isis created a phallus of gold and sang about Osiris and by her magic he was momentarily restored and his last son, Horus, was conceived.

In this way, Osiris became the new lord of the underworld. When Isis knew she was pregnant she fled to the Nile delta to hide from jealous Set who would want to kill her son. When Horus grew to be a man, he defeated Set in battle, though Set gouged out his left eye. Horus's face was mostly repaired by Hathor, the goddess of love. Horus offered his left eye to Osiris, in hope of returning him to life. So the eye came to symbolize sacrifice, healing and restoration. Horus became the protector of pharaohs.

A Day Trip to El Alamein

The desert is full: small succulents, scorpions
Egyptian cobras, the horned viper –
and in the Commonwealth soldiers' cemetery
a garden of cacti thrives.
Elsewhere the war has not been tidied up –
buried men beside their half-buried machines.
A Spitfire, a ration tin, spent shell casings
a uniform with its soldier blown out.
Here lies a sergeant of this war, known unto God.

El Alamein: a battlefield that is all museum
(until the day those luxury beachside condos are finished).

On our way back to Cairo
we slow for hundreds of sheep crossing
and a Bedouin herder, who allows us to take his picture.
This long, pristine asphalt ribbon
leads to the most crowded
city in the world: the triumphal, the ancient Misr.
I feel a small purification in these myths
then lose it all at the sight of our tour representative
and our driver, whose eyes
grip the road, his gaze as steely
as his new tires.

We do not have forty days to spare for fasting
or time to stop and purge behind the rear bumper –
we have only a photo of a soldier's cross
while solitude, sun and sand remake the world
ecstatic and thin. I ignore repeated offers to stop
for bottled water, allegedly imported
from foreign places like Canada. I will draw
on my internal fats and minerals
until I shed my bitterness
like a snake's skin
against that rock.

Top Deck Lounge

The glass surface of a wicker table
reflects me in a new light.
A waiter hovers, immaculate in white shirt and bow tie.
Sir, I have a message for you . . .

He is bound to his role
and I cannot leave this ship either.
Though I'm the one he tries to please –
in a few days I'll be able to travel away
while he cannot get a visa to Canada or America.

We have sailed the itinerary of jollity and monotony. And all it costs
is money and our dignity – what we can and can't take with us.
I am unable to play my role, and order
a brandy and a cigarette. The golden everything:
my passport and wallet, worth so much more here in Egypt than at home.

Confused by his exaggerated courtesy
my bliss shatters. Before we left Canada, Rameez warned me
You're not prepared for the Third World. It's not like Europe,
full of people like you.
I remember books by F. Scott Fitzgerald
and a Rockefeller who said, *The only thing*
that gives me pleasure is to see
my dividends come in.

God of Money, help your novice. How much should I tip?

Inflight Movie, No Headphones

Everything comes from above –
the food, the movie, the emergency oxygen.

Icy Greenland below
is but a garnish on the constant cold
from the air conditioning.
We've been sealed in this shiny cylinder
and hear the jet muffle of an ongoing
controlled explosion.

Too stroppy and bleary-eyed to read
I can only watch David Duchovny
scamper from one collapsing building to another.

Too tired for the free headphones I remain
blissfully deaf to dialogue.
Only the sight gags work. The fireman
throws a female dummy into a shack
sets it on fire, then practises breaking in
dragging her out, throwing her to the ground
and applying mouth-to-mouth to her straw body
half-blazing.

And the obvious casting – *X-Files* star
to investigate a pattern of meteors
crashing in Arizona. As an airborne phenomenon
myself, I appreciate how we gloss over the moment
of purifying flames, the impact – let's go straight to defeating
the muck-monsters from the special effects department.
Duchovny kisses the girl,
and his friend, the fireman
gets to drive his slime-splattered truck down Main Street
to the parade, the medal ceremony and
a brass band. The girl's hair and makeup
are fantastic, untouched by conflict.

Something else to look forward to on Earth.

Redrawn
Gestures

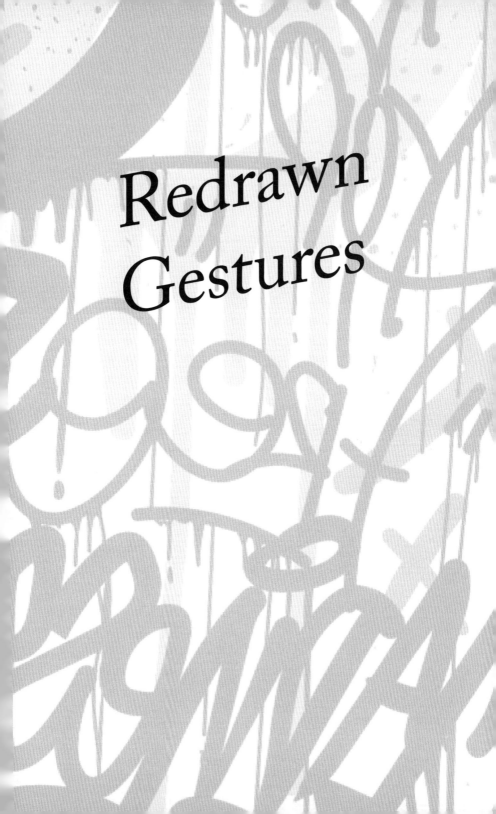

Comic Book Darkness

hair of bat
web of spider
speed of lizard
stealth of cat

bullet   claw
      spike   and blade
deceit of poison   mere prick

Shakespeare would have used tainted fencers' foils
but with these drawn and redrawn gestures
      figures slash
      and drops swell into a crimson flood

fear makes me sweat
makes a fetid unbathed city
real on the bus, where they might
be reading over my shoulder

the body releases the blade back to the killer
the skin peels back   blood thickens
too rich   too thick to be real
tendons melt
      unhook the muscles to the floor

this night   the premonition of a knife tear
or a bullet punching in
                total shock
to never feel that part of my body again

     the constant
threat against some life

someone's brooding for the courage
to kill, something best done at night
in the rain

Mind Swapping

Best if done between opposites.
Can have fatal side effects due to unstable technology.

Ambitious but sickly genius seeks virile he-man body.
Applicant should be a brutish thug who's none too bright.
Must be willing to lie down on a table covered with wires
wear a metal cap plugged into an electrical panel.
I'm doing this to make you smarter.
I'll lie beside you and some of my intellect will be transferred to you.

Suddenly the dumb guy's trapped in the weak guy's body
and so are the readers. Two villains
one dire situation. No hero at hand.
Equipment gets trashed. Impossible to escape
or reverse the procedure.

Or you might want to exact your revenge on the hero
by swapping bodies with him. Because he's smart
and wary of you, you're going to need
something that works without wires
some mystical mumbo-jumbo or a new source of gamma ray energy.
I recommend being lost in outer space for a while,
then move in with a race of short ugly aliens
who can switch bodies by mental power alone.
Learn how they do it, then zip back to Earth.

Now get into a little hand-to-hand scrap
with your nemesis and pull the old switcheroo.
Toss your rival (your body)
in a closet somewhere. Kiss his girlfriend,
rummage through his laboratory, empty his bank account
which regrettably holds very little
since he's been spending every spare dime
on chemistry equipment
and door frames for inter-dimensional portals.

People treat you nice, because they think you're him.
You start to like it, you wonder
about that conquering mankind thing,
that hatred you've nursed ever since the accident that turned you
into a disfigured evil genius. You look so handsome now
and his inter-dimensional portal looks cool.
You want to try it, without a return ticket.

The Hardy Days of Change

"Never mind the jokes, young man. Features do reveal character." Miss Hardy asked for pencil and paper and sketched the intruder's ears. She added, "He was about five feet eight, blond, broad-shouldered, and had a tooth missing in front."
– Franklin W. Dixon, *A Figure in Hiding*

One morning we awoke with an ache and knew we had lost track of the trees that we'd climbed and the binoculars with which we'd gazed upon a world so large and distant, we wept for joy when we saw it.

Now that distant tower and its treasure are gone. You see us as comical figures in the orange or brown endpapers of our books. Up a tree or crouched behind bushes, frozen in adolescence, spying on someone.

We had been raised in the heroic mode. We sought the approval of our father and thought that following in his size twelve footsteps would show us the way through life. Taking action and collecting clues (in the embers, in the sound of screeching owls) comforted us, like our mother's smile and gentle touch as she served us dinner, and then dessert, and then implored us not to take risks while hunting for hidden gold. Like that view from the trees, she was clear, unambiguous.

With a brother close in age, who might have been named Frank or with friends like Chet and Biff, we would unthinkingly stick up for those in distress, just as the police were always helpful, no matter the trouble, no matter what far-off town we found ourselves in, for every policeman knew our father, Fenton, as one of them, trustworthy men of honour.

Our greatest sins were committed against the girls: Callie and Iola and the others we left behind as we solved those mysteries – of Cabin Island, of the yellow feather, of the Flying Express – as we embraced adventure. How did they tolerate being trapped in our stories, admired for their purity and common sense? Their good hearts always made counterpoint to the villains that surrounded us. They baked muffins, sewed shirts that had been torn in hand-to-hand combat, and while we were gone – lost in a criss-cross shadow, or stowed away on a phantom freighter – they or our mother would receive cryptic telegrams about us, secret warnings.

Though we were living larger than our seventeen and eighteen years, anyone could have been fair-haired and dark-haired like us, amateur sleuths, abducted, assaulted or abandoned along the roads, fields and in derelict farmhouses of the great northeast. Life was easy and tolerable as we carried on against thugs, thieves and threats to national security. Our boat and our car were tampered with so often, I wonder how they were always restored to us in the nick of time, whenever we needed them, by a mechanic in a nearby garage who just happened to have the right part – for we had so many bad men to overcome, escort from the story and dispatch into justice.

The Beach Boys Singing

The daughters of muses had come down
from their mothers in the mountains
to savour the sun and the salty air
             but accidentally
embodied their own vinyl permanence.

What stylist knew what to do
with all that blond hair?
On album sleeves, in super-8 movies
how clear they seem, alive in the eye –
eternally girlish. They could only have sprung from
young male voices.

How Greek, how perfectly posed –
desire made as real as a painting, an urn,
             a sunlit wall.
A rebellious boy runs his hand across a statue
as if to say that art will have to do.
The boys by the bay – all tremor and adrenaline –
with their harmonies and high tenor voices they illuminate
the audience, from rhythm rises a sweet haze
so they and their audience might escape those they long for –
that's why Elvis left the building.

The girls seem assured and will never deny
they've enchanted these boys, as Circe once
turned seamen to swine.

Or perhaps they'll
be loved like Persephone – six months in the sun.
Suffering Hades the rest of the year.
Where all was cold. Where no gentle breeze, romantic stars
or a growing rose, ever inspired a song
or a boy to sing one.

An Ambitious Young Man

1.

I quit the job
after thinking too much of your eyes and hair
after inhaling your despair, I wanted to grow
a goatee, put my long hair in a ponytail
read in public, excruciatingly slowly.

I quit the job
because you accept eighty percent slavery
on the dollar and are still beautiful.

Go buy Leonard Cohen, love –
go buy books by my English professor.
Don't dignify your poverty, no matter how many
PR men spread their beautiful suit jackets
over puddles for you.
My memory overflows with shredded
memos, old trade deals and trickery –
I can't help but miss your shiny words.

I'm going to eastern Europe with my guitar
and old Dylan records. I'll make mediocre money
and come back arrogant, knowing I have a future
shouting from stages and praising other writers
to their faces though they whine

and spill drunken complaints
about editors and former friends –
I want them to like me.

2.
Didn't say where I'd go
but I'm certain I'm gone now
took six months just to get my parachute untangled
lucky this was solid ground
when I landed here, wherever I am.

Most of my life, my map's been upside down
the bridges of Bothersome County all lead to
the road not taken, but there's a reason I don't know yet –
we'll fall off that bridge when we get to it.

This is just to say, I'm not William Carlos Williams
and the pizza's gone stale in the fridge.
I'm not bitter, well maybe a little
but it was my decision.

I'd love to blame you but I can't.
Can't blame my family or the government
I didn't think much about leaving, it just happened.
Wish you were here
I mean it.

Upon Hearing "Strangers in the Night" on an Accordion as We Sat in an Outdoor Café at Quarter to Two in the Afternoon

Cobblestones incline
beneath our feet, the slopes of Lisbon
serve us the smell of french fries and overheard accents
swoop in from Britain and America. But also
Italian, African, Dutch, French
and Polish chatters around and around
this warm green umbrella.

A tiny truck, two scooters, a golf cart for deliveries –
motorize the constant push of pedestrians to pass
out of step with puttering mini-taxis
that ply the way of narrow Serpa Pinto –
outside the next café a statue of young Fernando
Pessoa sits at a bronze desk
in a suit favoured by the older James
Joyce.

Now having exhausted Frank Sinatra's signature tune
the player begins a vigorous version of "Those Were the Days"
my friend, we think he will never end, his tempo, a march
he sways and sweats, and nothing withstands the performance:
not Mary Hopkin, not Lennon-McCartney
or the Russian folk song they swiped, long, long ago.

The most handsome of the four waiters
with his cleft chin, his tan, his white shirt, black pants and apron –
and, oh, his sunglasses. He could be a film star. Three American girls
four tables over, vie for his attention. They're on a holiday thanks to
the recent decline in the euro, the Greek debt crisis, you know.
But the wrong waiter –
the pudgy one – is waiting. They pout.

I'm thinking we should go. You wink, you agree –
behind me one matron complains to another about her husband,
speaks primly in Portuguese, then the words *bastard*
and *workaholic* break through.

The Difficulty of Photographs

1.

You've burnt some popcorn
I've spilled some red wine
Beethoven fades out on the radio
on another station, a faint hockey game
two small trees cross trunks and squeak
beyond the cabin wall.

October ghosts drop snow
across the Lake of Bays at dusk.
This morning's leaves still burn
yellow and orange in memory.
We discuss the difficulty of photographs,
how technology reduces
green spruces to lines
above burning colours.
Pleased with the weather and camera
we try to frame the maple and birch
that have taken the place of many thousands
of giant white and red pines cut for Queen Victoria's navy.
A logger would take down three hundred years of growth
in thirty minutes, when the land was blue with pine.

2.

We cruise under
a golden canopy of leaves
in our steel blue car,
eye the signs and stories of development
the vanished logging towns –
Tom Thomson drowned at Canoe Lake
his vision bursting, his mind in flames. We wouldn't
saw a Group of Seven painting in half,
but having slowly exterminated the wolves in Ontario
he's all we have left,
the tragic artist pops up as a visual aid.
The Algonquin Park guidebook clears its throat
points to an archival logging-railroad-whistle-rifle-shot
photograph of twenty orderly corpses,
foxes, like rags on a clothesline.

3.
Suddenly: Shidane Arone.
I was supposed to forget
the sixteen trophy photographs
his bloody swollen face,
his broken ribs and endless
crucifying death.
I was supposed to forget
the defence minister's denial
the promise to investigate
the blind generals who faded out
like radio at a distance
like the Romans after Golgotha,
their static complexities
unchanged. Brief press briefings,
then a commercial for a car in the Rockies.
I was supposed to shrug at military games.
Our boys.

We slur the warm red remains in the glass,
popcorn burnt down to the hard kernels
the play-by-play of the game far away.

Gravity tugs the half-cut tree
we pirouette drunkenly
without a painting of the wild,
blind to photographs
wet with blood, unable to mourn
what we have eliminated
from earth, the coming cold.

Cedar

I always made an awkward bow.
– John Keats, final letter to Charles Brown

A forest seems a pleasant place to fall
among cedar and spruce, some few
browning branches and yellowing leaves of grass.
When you know the deceased
you feel what a cedar coffin
bluntly teaches.

Otherwise, a funeral home pretends a grief
it doesn't know, to keep up appearances, as if the mourners
are imposters, as if we were all just curtains and flowers.
Take your cue from the calm deportment
of the staff. Church bells summon us –
be still.

We promise to remember the war dead
        yet only photography is forever.
The few faces my father showed me of family
of handsome boys and girls in uniform
are no more, relations
and yet, unknown.

My father who knew them
is gone. The letters he and my mother wrote
were mailed. Here are the multitude they received:
blue aerogrammes from the post office of sadness
mundane news from another time.

The letters of young recruits say they'll be home soon.
Optimists, like rookie journalists, vulnerable
to newsprint and its failure to endure the sun, the air
and time.
No one able to step into the same war twice.
Many exit with no bow at all.

His Grandmother's Clock

He was near dying, his doctors uncertain
So many maladies harboured in him, a heart worn down
by time and now liver disease
only a full head of white hair belying
these signs of his age

Every few days, with its burnished bronze key
old David would wind the clock. And it began
again to move, but after an hour it would stop –
                  unsprung as before

The repairman, a youngster named Clem
in the business of watches, came by and with
much hemming about all the clock's delicate metal parts
set it working, but
within an hour of Clem's leaving
the clock had stopped again
as if it grieved all the time it had hung on the wall
in a form that witnessed all the members
of the house –
                passing away –
through the front door –
on gurneys, crutches or under their own steam

Reliant only on the twist
of old David's wrist
having served the family over two hundred years
his grandmother's clock –

       its deeply dark rich wood stronger than ever
       in a glass cabinet perfectly preserved –
had finally settled on the correct signal to its final heir
the end of keeping time was near

Listening

for David Haskins

Your latest email
speaks with your voice –
the joking and worry blend,
though lately, over the phone, you were
all whispery rasp, from intubation
at the hospital.

Into the medical system you went
for an erratic heartbeat, blood pressure falling through
the floor, another chance for your doctor
to fool with your medications –
only thirteen pills a day now
down from sixteen, two weeks ago

Is this your time? Will you leave us
of a sudden?
I don't suppose you know –
the hospital monitor thinks of you as
a series of data points. I know the author of your poems.
There was no retirement from writing
or teaching for that matter.
You received the pension of an English head.
You continue to be afflicted by words.

Your Bee Gees allusions
"How Can You Mend a Broken Heart"
and "Stayin' Alive." Yes, now's the time
to laugh. Sometimes we go
against the grain, create a mess
in lines of shovelled snow.
Illness does not prevent the ear
from hearing the inaudible –
the better life –
the one we don't yet know.

Acknowledgements

Many thanks to my editor, Maureen Hynes, for helping to shape this book and many of the individual poems as they now appear.

Additional good advice was received from Richard Harrison, Allan Briesmaster, Shane Neilson and members of the Emmanuel College Workshop (attended by John Reibetanz, Sue Chenette, KD Miller, Carla Hartsfield and others).

A few of these poems were originally published in a chapbook from The Alfred Gustav Press, edited by David Zieroth: "The Nile," "By the Portrait of a Polish Nobleman" and "Inflight Movie, No Headphones."

Other poems were published in the *South Shore Review*, the *Hearthbeat* anthology (ed. Don Gutteridge), the *Tamaracks* anthology (ed. James Deahl), *The Beauty of Being Elsewhere* (ed. John B. Lee) and *Hamilton Arts & Letters* (eds. Paul Lisson and Fiona Kinsella). My thanks to the editors of those publications.

For their ongoing support of my writing and their interest in poetry at large I thank Noelle Allen, Ashley Hisson, Jennifer Rawlinson and Tania Blokhuis at Wolsak and Wynn Publishers. As well, my late friends David Haskins and Andrew Arntfield have offered encouragement and support along the way.

This collection is dedicated to my wife, Janice Jackson, and my brothers, Justin and Adrian, and my sister, Moira.

Notes

Le Lit (The Bed)

In English, *The Bed* as viewed in Paris, circa 2011.

"Musée d'Orsay is a museum on the Left Bank of the Seine. It is housed in the former Gare d'Orsay, a Beaux-Arts railway station built between 1898 and 1900. The museum holds mainly French art dating from 1848 to 1914, including paintings, sculptures, furniture, and photography." (Source: "Musée d'Orsay," Wikipedia.)

Water Lilies

"*Water Lilies* (or *Nymphéas*) is a series of approximately 250 oil paintings by Claude Monet (1840–1926)." (Source: "*Water Lilies* [Monet series]," Wikipedia.)

"Musée de l'Orangerie . . . is an art gallery of impressionist and post-impressionist paintings located in the west corner of the Tuileries Garden next to the Place de la Concorde in Paris." (Source: "Musée de l'Orangerie," Wikipedia.)

How We Fear Each Other

DARTS is an acronym of Disabled and Aged Regional Transit System, a transportation service operating in Hamilton for passengers who face significant difficulties using public transit.

One Morning, One Afternoon

Billy Collins was poet laureate of the USA from 2001 to 2003.

In the beginning,

The story of Isis and Osiris is a foundational tale anchoring many other stories within Egyptian mythology. Like many tales that deal with the origins of the Earth or the Egyptian people and empire, there are many versions of the story of this relationship and there is little scholarly agreement on which version of Isis's efforts to restore Osiris to life should take precedence. Details used in the poem were provided by guides in Egypt in 2005 and supported by various Wikipedia articles.

The Hardy Days of Change

Franklin W. Dixon is the pseudonym used by various ghostwriters of boys' adventures (*The Hardy Boys*) produced by the Stratemeyer Syndicate and published by Grosset & Dunlap in America beginning in 1927. Leslie McFarlane authored nineteen of the first twenty-five titles between 1927 and 1946. Unlike many other Syndicate ghostwriters, McFarlane was regarded highly enough by the Syndicate that he was frequently given advances of twenty-five or fifty dollars. During the Depression, when fees were lowered, he was paid eighty-five dollars for each *Hardy Boys* book when other Syndicate ghostwriters were receiving only seventy-five dollars for their productions. According to McFarlane's family, he despised the series and its characters.

The original *Hardy Boys* series ended in 2005. Further information on the titles mentioned in the poem can be found on Wikipedia under the article "The Hardy Boys." See also: Deirdre Johnson, *Edward Stratemeyer and the Stratemeyer Syndicate* (New York: Twayne, 1993).

An Ambitious Young Man

References to bestselling books during the 1990s: *What Color Is Your Parachute?* (Richard N. Bolles), *The Bridges of Madison County* (Robert James Waller) and *The Road Less Traveled* (M. Scott Peck).

Also, the poem glances at two of the most famous twentieth-century American poems: Robert Frost's "The Road Not Taken" and William Carlos Williams's "This Is Just to Say."

Upon Hearing "Strangers in the Night" on an Accordion . . .

Mary Hopkin was a singer and protege of Paul McCartney. In 1968, she had a major hit with "Those Were the Days" for The Beatles' record label Apple. Fernando Pessoa (1888–1935) is generally viewed as one of the most significant literary figures of the twentieth century and one of the greatest poets in the Portuguese language.

The Difficulty of Photographs

A detailed online summary of the circumstances in which the Somali teenager Shidane Arone was tortured and murdered by soldiers in the Canadian Airborne Regiment in 1993 is available in the Wikipedia article "Somalia Affair."

Chris Pannell has published seven previous books of poetry; his last was titled *The Fragmentarium and Other Poems* (2022). *A Nervous City* (2013) won the Kerry Schooley Book Award from the Hamilton Arts Council. *Love, Despite the Ache* (2016) won Hamilton Literary Award for Poetry from the Hamilton Arts Council. *Drive* (2009) won the Acorn-Plantos Award in 2010. Pannell is also the author of a set of three poetry broadsheets (*Fractures, Subluxations & Dislocations*), which won the Hamilton and Region Arts Council Award in 1997.

He is a former DARTS bus driver, a former technical writer and has hosted and helped run the Lit Live Reading Series in Hamilton for twenty years. From 1993 to 2005 he ran the new writing workshop at Hamilton Artists Inc. and edited two book-length anthologies for the group.